This Book Belongs To:

_____

_____

_____

JOURNAL for the book
Self-Aware: A Guide for Success in Work and Life

Copyright and Contact Info
For more information on my Personal Development Plan series,
visit http://RobPasick.com

ISBN-13: 978-1979787468

You may contact the author at Rob@robpasick.com

Introduction

Welcome to the Self-Aware Journal. This journal is designed to help you develop and enhance your self awareness. The format and content of the journal Is one that I have created, based on my over forty years as a psychologist, as well as three years teaching at the University of Michigan.

My goal is a simple one: to share a process to help you improve yourself.

The process also is simple.

- Start by setting two school or career and two personal goals for
    - ninety days,
    - one year, and
    - three years
- Next, begin to use your Self-Aware Journal on a daily basis.
    - There are ninety-one days in the journal, one for each day of the quarter.
    - Each day you will be asked to do eight tasks.

Here are the directions for the eight tasks:

1. On the left side of the journal, answer the question, "What will make today a great day?"

2. Next, fill out all scheduled hours of the day
    a. On the right side of the appointment entry for each hour scheduled, write what you intend to achieve during this hour.
    b. On the left side of the journal, write any action item that comes out of the meeting or class. By action, I mean something that you have committed to do as a result of the meeting or an idea you intend to pursue.

3. As the day proceeds, fill in the blank hours by what you intend to do with that time.

4. You are asked to set at most three goals for each day, no more but it could be less.

5. First list the most important goal. If possible, start your free time by working on the number one goal.

6. Next. move on to the right hand side of the page.

7. Keep track of the gratitudes of your day. Some examples:

   - When someone has been nice to you
   - When you've done someone a favor
   - You had a special moment
   - A meeting or class has gone particularly well
   - You have overcome the fear
   - You received good news about a friend or family member
   - When you've offered someone praise or encouragement
   - You receive praise or encouragement
   - You had an achievement, however small
   - You noticed something beautiful or meaningful
   - Or anything else that you are grateful for, appreciate, or enjoy

8. After the three goals, you will find a quote from my book, Self-Aware: A Guide for Success in Work and Life https://www.amazon.com/dp/B01LFZR5Z6/. The quote directs you to either reflect on a particular thing about yourself or to take a specific action to help you learn more about yourself. If you need more space, there are blank pages in the back of the book where you can write more about your daily reflections.

9. Next, you are asked to reflect on lessons about yourself that you have learned during the day. In the "Lessons Learned" section, reflect on what went well what did not go well during today and record what you are learning about how to do better tomorrow.

10. Lastly, record in your journal what you have done today to take good care of yourself and others in mind, body, and spirit.

....

Goals

....

90 Days

School Career Goals

Personal Goals

1 Year

School Career Goals

Personal Goals

3 Year

School Career Goals

Personal Goals

01	02	03	04	05	06	07	08	09	10	11	12

I will feel great about today if:

Appointments	Intent	Action
7:00		
8:00		
9:00		
10:00		
11:00		
12:00		
1:00		
2:00		
3:00		
4:00		
5:00		
6:00		

Top three tasks and top priority for today

1.

2.

3.

Gratitudes

Today's self-awareness exercise

Today, track what gives you energy and makes you feel joy.

Life Lessons Learned (L3)

Take Good Care of Self and Others (TGCoSO)

Self	Others

01	02	03	04	05	06	07	08	09	10	11	12

I will feel great about today if:

Appointments	Intent	Action
7:00		
8:00		
9:00		
10:00		
11:00		
12:00		
1:00		
2:00		
3:00		
4:00		
5:00		
6:00		

Top three tasks and top priority for today

1.

2.

3.

Gratitudes

Today's self-awareness exercise

List what you think your top three strengths are.

Life Lessons Learned (L3)

Take Good Care of Self and Others (TGCoSO)

Self	Others

| 01 | 02 | 03 | 04 | 05 | 06 | 07 | 08 | 09 | 10 | 11 | 12 |

I will feel great about today if:

Appointments | Intent | Action

7:00 —————————

8:00 —————————

9:00 —————————

10:00 —————————

11:00 —————————

12:00 —————————

1:00 —————————

2:00 —————————

3:00 —————————

4:00 —————————

5:00 —————————

6:00 —————————

Top three tasks and top priority for today

1. _____

2. _____

3. _____

Gratitudes

Today's self-awareness exercise

Watch Rob's video on emotional intelligence https://youtu.be/4Qfx_aFLfhw

Life Lessons Learned (L3)

Take Good Care of Self and Others (TGCoSO)

Self	Others

01	02	03	04	05	06	07	08	09	10	11	12

I will feel great about today if:

Appointments   Intent   Action

7:00

8:00

9:00

10:00

11:00

12:00

1:00

2:00

3:00

4:00

5:00

6:00

Top three tasks and top priority for today

1.

2.

3.

Gratitudes

Today's self-awareness exercise

Ask a friend or family member what they see as your best qualities and strengths.

Life Lessons Learned (L3)

Take Good Care of Self and Others (TGCoSO)

Self	Others

01	02	03	04	05	06	07	08	09	10	11	12

I will feel great about today if:

Appointments	Intent	Action
7:00		
8:00		
9:00		
10:00		
11:00		
12:00		
1:00		
2:00		
3:00		
4:00		
5:00		
6:00		

Top three tasks and top priority for today

1.

2.

3.

01 02 03 04 05 06 07 08 09 10 11 12 13 14 15 16 17 18 19 20 21 22 23 24 25 26 27 28 29 30 31

Gratitudes

Today's self-awareness exercise

Reflect on what you care about deeply, and ask yourself, why?

Life Lessons Learned (L3)

_____

_____

_____

Take Good Care of Self and Others (TGCoSO)

Self	Others

I will feel great about today if:

Appointments	Intent	Action
7:00		
8:00		
9:00		
10:00		
11:00		
12:00		
1:00		
2:00		
3:00		
4:00		
5:00		
6:00		

Top three tasks and top priority for today

1.

2.

3.

Gratitudes

Today's self-awareness exercise

Reflect a societal problem for which you would like to contribute a solution?

Life Lessons Learned (L3)

Take Good Care of Self and Others (TGCoSO)

Self	Others

01	02	03	04	05	06	07	08	09	10	11	12

I will feel great about today if:

Appointments	Intent	Action
7:00		
8:00		
9:00		
10:00		
11:00		
12:00		
1:00		
2:00		
3:00		
4:00		
5:00		
6:00		

Top three tasks and top priority for today

1.

2.

3.

Gratitudes

Today's self-awareness exercise
Anything worth achieving requires facing distinct difficulties, experiencing internal struggle, and accepting big risk.

Life Lessons Learned (L3)

Take Good Care of Self and Others (TGCoSO)

Self	Others

INTENTION

| 01 | 02 | 03 | 04 | 05 | 06 | 07 | 08 | 09 | 10 | 11 | 12 |

I will feel great about today if:

Appointments   Intent   Action

7:00

8:00

9:00

10:00

11:00

12:00

1:00

2:00

3:00

4:00

5:00

6:00

Top three tasks and top priority for today

1.

2.

3.

Gratitudes

Today's self-awareness exercise

For what are you willing to take a big risk?

Life Lessons Learned (L3)

Take Good Care of Self and Others (TGCoSO)

Self	Others

I will feel great about today if:

Appointments   Intent   Action

7:00 ———————————   ———————————   ———————————

8:00 ———————————   ———————————   ———————————

9:00 ———————————   ———————————   ———————————

10:00 ———————————   ———————————   ———————————

11:00 ———————————   ———————————   ———————————

12:00 ———————————   ———————————   ———————————

1:00 ———————————   ———————————   ———————————

2:00 ———————————   ———————————   ———————————

3:00 ———————————   ———————————   ———————————

4:00 ———————————   ———————————   ———————————

5:00 ———————————   ———————————   ———————————

6:00 ———————————   ———————————   ———————————

Top three tasks and top priority for today

1. _____

2. _____

3. _____

Gratitudes

Today's self-awareness exercise

What did you love to do as a child that you're not doing enough of now?

Life Lessons Learned (L3)

Take Good Care of Self and Others (TGCoSO)

Self	Others

01	02	03	04	05	06	07	08	09	10	11	12

I will feel great about today if:

Appointments   Intent   Action

7:00

8:00

9:00

10:00

11:00

12:00

1:00

2:00

3:00

4:00

5:00

6:00

Top three tasks and top priority for today

1.

2.

3.

Gratitudes

Today's self-awareness exercise

What did you think you were going to be when you "grew up"?

Life Lessons Learned (L3)

Take Good Care of Self and Others (TGCoSO)

Self	Others

I will feel great about today if:

Appointments   Intent   Action

7:00 ——————————————   ——————————————   ——————————————

8:00 ——————————————   ——————————————   ——————————————

9:00 ——————————————   ——————————————   ——————————————

10:00 ——————————————   ——————————————   ——————————————

11:00 ——————————————   ——————————————   ——————————————

12:00 ——————————————   ——————————————   ——————————————

1:00 ——————————————   ——————————————   ——————————————

2:00 ——————————————   ——————————————   ——————————————

3:00 ——————————————   ——————————————   ——————————————

4:00 ——————————————   ——————————————   ——————————————

5:00 ——————————————   ——————————————   ——————————————

6:00 ——————————————   ——————————————   ——————————————

Top three tasks and top priority for today

1. ——

2. ——

3. ——

Gratitudes

Today's self-awareness exercise

What gets you up with enthusiasm in the morning?

Life Lessons Learned (L3)

Take Good Care of Self and Others (TGCoSO)

Self	Others

| 01 | 02 | 03 | 04 | 05 | 06 | 07 | 08 | 09 | 10 | 11 | 12 |

I will feel great about today if:

Appointments	Intent	Action
7:00		
8:00		
9:00		
10:00		
11:00		
12:00		
1:00		
2:00		
3:00		
4:00		
5:00		
6:00		

Top three tasks and top priority for today

1.

2.

3.

Gratitudes

Today's self-awareness exercise

What type of conversations engage you?

Life Lessons Learned (L3)

Take Good Care of Self and Others (TGCoSO)

Self	Others

| 01 | 02 | 03 | 04 | 05 | 06 | 07 | 08 | 09 | 10 | 11 | 12 |

I will feel great about today if:

Appointments   Intent   Action

7:00

8:00

9:00

10:00

11:00

12:00

1:00

2:00

3:00

4:00

5:00

6:00

Top three tasks and top priority for today

1.

2.

3.

Gratitudes

Today's self-awareness exercise

What brings you the most joy in life?

Life Lessons Learned (L3)

Take Good Care of Self and Others (TGCoSO)

Self	Others

01	02	03	04	05	06	07	08	09	10	11	12

I will feel great about today if:

Appointments	Intent	Action

7:00 ———————————

8:00 ———————————

9:00 ———————————

10:00 ———————————

11:00 ———————————

12:00 ———————————

1:00 ———————————

2:00 ———————————

3:00 ———————————

4:00 ———————————

5:00 ———————————

6:00 ———————————

Top three tasks and top priority for today

1. ————————————————

2. ————————————————

3. ————————————————

Gratitudes

Today's self-awareness exercise

When you have had a great day, what was it you were doing and what are you not doing?

Life Lessons Learned (L3)

_____

_____

_____

Take Good Care of Self and Others (TGCoSO)

Self	Others

01	02	03	04	05	06	07	08	09	10	11	12

I will feel great about today if:

Appointments | Intent | Action

7:00

8:00

9:00

10:00

11:00

12:00

1:00

2:00

3:00

4:00

5:00

6:00

Top three tasks and top priority for today

1.

2.

3.

Gratitudes

Today's self-awareness exercise

Passion is about emotion. What topic most evokes a strong emotional reaction in you?

Life Lessons Learned (L3)

Take Good Care of Self and Others (TGCoSO)

Self	Others

| 01 | 02 | 03 | 04 | 05 | 06 | 07 | 08 | 09 | 10 | 11 | 12 |

I will feel great about today if:

Appointments   Intent   Action

7:00

8:00

9:00

10:00

11:00

12:00

1:00

2:00

3:00

4:00

5:00

6:00

Top three tasks and top priority for today

1.

2.

3.

01 02 03 04 05 06 07 08 09 10 11 12 13 14 15 16 17 18 19 20 21 22 23 24 25 26 27 28 29 30 31

Gratitudes

Today's self-awareness exercise

What do you love to do with your free time?

Life Lessons Learned (L3)

Take Good Care of Self and Others (TGCoSO)

Self	Others

01	02	03	04	05	06	07	08	09	10	11	12

I will feel great about today if:

Appointments · Intent · Action

7:00

8:00

9:00

10:00

11:00

12:00

1:00

2:00

3:00

4:00

5:00

6:00

Top three tasks and top priority for today

1.

2.

3.

Gratitudes

Today's self-awareness exercise
Even if you were not getting paid for it, what occupational activities would you be willing to do for free?

Life Lessons Learned (L3)

Take Good Care of Self and Others (TGCoSO)

Self	Others

I will feel great about today if:

Appointments   Intent   Action

7:00 ——————————   ——————————   ——————————

8:00 ——————————   ——————————   ——————————

9:00 ——————————   ——————————   ——————————

10:00 ——————————   ——————————   ——————————

11:00 ——————————   ——————————   ——————————

12:00 ——————————   ——————————   ——————————

1:00 ——————————   ——————————   ——————————

2:00 ——————————   ——————————   ——————————

3:00 ——————————   ——————————   ——————————

4:00 ——————————   ——————————   ——————————

5:00 ——————————   ——————————   ——————————

6:00 ——————————   ——————————   ——————————

Top three tasks and top priority for today

1. _____

2. _____

3. _____

01 02 03 04 05 06 07 08 09 10 11 12 13 14 15 16 17 18 19 20 21 22 23 24 25 26 27 28 29 30 31

Gratitudes

Today's self-awareness exercise

Create a "passion masterpiece" such as a scrapbook or poster.

Life Lessons Learned (L3)

Take Good Care of Self and Others (TGCoSO)

Self	Others

01	02	03	04	05	06	07	08	09	10	11	12

I will feel great about today if:

Appointments   Intent   Action

7:00 _____   _____   _____

8:00 _____   _____   _____

9:00 _____   _____   _____

10:00 _____   _____   _____

11:00 _____   _____   _____

12:00 _____   _____   _____

1:00 _____   _____   _____

2:00 _____   _____   _____

3:00 _____   _____   _____

4:00 _____   _____   _____

5:00 _____   _____   _____

6:00 _____   _____   _____

Top three tasks and top priority for today

1. _____

2. _____

3. _____

01 02 03 04 05 06 07 08 09 10 11 12 13 14 15 16 17 18 19 20 21 22 23 24 25 26 27 28 29 30 31

Gratitudes

Today's self-awareness exercise

What disciplines or subject did you dislike in school and why?

Life Lessons Learned (L3)

Take Good Care of Self and Others (TGCoSO)

Self	Others

01	02	03	04	05	06	07	08	09	10	11	12

I will feel great about today if:

Appointments	Intent	Action
7:00		
8:00		
9:00		
10:00		
11:00		
12:00		
1:00		
2:00		
3:00		
4:00		
5:00		
6:00		

Top three tasks and top priority for today

1.

2.

3.

Gratitudes

Today's self-awareness exercise

What kinds of tasks and activities do you find you typically put off?

Life Lessons Learned (L3)

Take Good Care of Self and Others (TGCoSO)

Self	Others

I will feel great about today if:

Appointments   Intent   Action

7:00 ———————— ———————— ————————

8:00 ———————— ———————— ————————

9:00 ———————— ———————— ————————

10:00 ———————— ———————— ————————

11:00 ———————— ———————— ————————

12:00 ———————— ———————— ————————

1:00 ———————— ———————— ————————

2:00 ———————— ———————— ————————

3:00 ———————— ———————— ————————

4:00 ———————— ———————— ————————

5:00 ———————— ———————— ————————

6:00 ———————— ———————— ————————

Top three tasks and top priority for today

1. ——————————————————————————————

2. ——————————————————————————————

3. ——————————————————————————————

Gratitudes

Today's self-awareness exercise

What are the tasks or activities that leave you very tired at the end of the day?

Life Lessons Learned (L3)

Take Good Care of Self and Others (TGCoSO)

Self	Others

01 **02** **03** **04** **05** **06** **07** **08** **09** **10** **11** **12**

I will feel great about today if:

Appointments	Intent	Action
7:00		
8:00		
9:00		
10:00		
11:00		
12:00		
1:00		
2:00		
3:00		
4:00		
5:00		
6:00		

Top three tasks and top priority for today

1.

2.

3.

Gratitudes

Today's self-awareness exercise

What takes the wind out of your sails?

Life Lessons Learned (L3)

Take Good Care of Self and Others (TGCoSO)

Self	Others

01	02	03	04	05	06	07	08	09	10	11	12

I will feel great about today if:

Appointments   Intent   Action

7:00 ——————

8:00 ——————

9:00 ——————

10:00 ——————

11:00 ——————

12:00 ——————

1:00 ——————

2:00 ——————

3:00 ——————

4:00 ——————

5:00 ——————

6:00 ——————

Top three tasks and top priority for today

1. _____

2. _____

3. _____

01 02 03 04 05 06 07 08 09 10 11 12 13 14 15 16 17 18 19 20 21 22 23 24 25 26 27 28 29 30 31

Gratitudes

Today's self-awareness exercise

What bores you?

Life Lessons Learned (L3)

Take Good Care of Self and Others (TGCoSO)

Self	Others

01	02	03	04	05	06	07	08	09	10	11	12

I will feel great about today if:

Appointments　　　　　　Intent　　　　　　Action

7:00

8:00

9:00

10:00

11:00

12:00

1:00

2:00

3:00

4:00

5:00

6:00

Top three tasks and top priority for today

1.

2.

3.

01 02 03 04 05 06 07 08 09 10 11 12 13 14 15 16 17 18 19 20 21 22 23 24 25 26 27 28 29 30 31

Gratitudes

Today's self-awareness exercise

What makes you feel limited or constrained?

Life Lessons Learned (L3)

Take Good Care of Self and Others (TGCoSO)

Self	Others

I will feel great about today if:

Appointments	Intent	Action
7:00		
8:00		
9:00		
10:00		
11:00		
12:00		
1:00		
2:00		
3:00		
4:00		
5:00		
6:00		

Top three tasks and top priority for today

1.

2.

3.

Gratitudes

Today's self-awareness exercise

Do you believe you can fundamentally improve yourself?

Life Lessons Learned (L3)

Take Good Care of Self and Others (TGCoSO)

Self	Others

I will feel great about today if:

Appointments	Intent	Action
7:00		
8:00		
9:00		
10:00		
11:00		
12:00		
1:00		
2:00		
3:00		
4:00		
5:00		
6:00		

Top three tasks and top priority for today

1.

2.

3.

01 02 03 04 05 06 07 08 09 10 11 12 13 14 15 16 17 18 19 20 21 22 23 24 25 26 27 28 29 30 31

Gratitudes

Today's self-awareness exercise

What have you quit or been fired from? Why?

Life Lessons Learned (L3)

Take Good Care of Self and Others (TGCoSO)

Self	Others

01	02	03	04	05	06	07	08	09	10	11	12

I will feel great about today if:

Appointments   Intent   Action

7:00 _____

8:00 _____

9:00 _____

10:00 _____

11:00 _____

12:00 _____

1:00 _____

2:00 _____

3:00 _____

4:00 _____

5:00 _____

6:00 _____

Top three tasks and top priority for today

1. _____

2. _____

3. _____

01 02 03 04 05 06 07 08 09 10 11 12 13 14 15 16 17 18 19 20 21 22 23 24 25 26 27 28 29 30 31

Gratitudes

Today's self-awareness exercise

Do you prefer change or keeping the status quo? Why?

Life Lessons Learned (L3)

Take Good Care of Self and Others (TGCoSO)

Self	Others

| 01 | 02 | 03 | 04 | 05 | 06 | 07 | 08 | 09 | 10 | 11 | 12 |

I will feel great about today if:

Appointments	Intent	Action
7:00		
8:00		
9:00		
10:00		
11:00		
12:00		
1:00		
2:00		
3:00		
4:00		
5:00		
6:00		

Top three tasks and top priority for today

1.

2.

3.

Gratitudes

Today's self-awareness exercise

Are you organized and disciplined?

Life Lessons Learned (L3)

Take Good Care of Self and Others (TGCoSO)

Self	Others

01	02	03	04	05	06	07	08	09	10	11	12

I will feel great about today if:

Appointments	Intent	Action
7:00		
8:00		
9:00		
10:00		
11:00		
12:00		
1:00		
2:00		
3:00		
4:00		
5:00		
6:00		

Top three tasks and top priority for today

1.

2.

3.

01 02 03 04 05 06 07 08 09 10 11 12 13 14 15 16 17 18 19 20 21 22 23 24 25 26 27 28 29 30 31

Gratitudes

Today's self-awareness exercise

Do you recharge yourself socially or alone?

Life Lessons Learned (L3)

Take Good Care of Self and Others (TGCoSO)

Self	Others

I will feel great about today if:

Appointments   Intent   Action

7:00

8:00

9:00

10:00

11:00

12:00

1:00

2:00

3:00

4:00

5:00

6:00

Top three tasks and top priority for today

1.

2.

3.

Gratitudes

Today's self-awareness exercise

Are you accommodating or firm?

Life Lessons Learned (L3)

Take Good Care of Self and Others (TGCoSO)

Self	Others

01	02	03	04	05	06	07	08	09	10	11	12

I will feel great about today if:

Appointments　　　　Intent　　　　Action

7:00

8:00

9:00

10:00

11:00

12:00

1:00

2:00

3:00

4:00

5:00

6:00

Top three tasks and top priority for today

1.

2.

3.

01 02 03 04 05 06 07 08 09 10 11 12 13 14 15 16 17 18 19 20 21 22 23 24 25 26 27 28 29 30 31

Gratitudes

Today's self-awareness exercise

You can't know your own blind spots. Ask others what they think your blind spots are.

Life Lessons Learned (L3)

Take Good Care of Self and Others (TGCoSO)

Self	Others

01	02	03	04	05	06	07	08	09	10	11	12

I will feel great about today if:

Appointments   Intent   Action

7:00

8:00

9:00

10:00

11:00

12:00

1:00

2:00

3:00

4:00

5:00

6:00

Top three tasks and top priority for today

1.

2.

3.

Gratitudes

Today's self-awareness exercise

Are you relaxed and calm or excitable / anxious?

Life Lessons Learned (L3)

Take Good Care of Self and Others (TGCoSO)

Self	Others

I will feel great about today if:

Appointments   Intent   Action

7:00 ————————————   ————————————   ————————————

8:00 ————————————   ————————————   ————————————

9:00 ————————————   ————————————   ————————————

10:00 ———————————   ————————————   ————————————

11:00 ———————————   ————————————   ————————————

12:00 ———————————   ————————————   ————————————

1:00 ————————————   ————————————   ————————————

2:00 ————————————   ————————————   ————————————

3:00 ————————————   ————————————   ————————————

4:00 ————————————   ————————————   ————————————

5:00 ————————————   ————————————   ————————————

6:00 ————————————   ————————————   ————————————

Top three tasks and top priority for today

1. ————————————————————————————————

2. ————————————————————————————————

3. ————————————————————————————————

Gratitudes

Today's self-awareness exercise

Identify the times you are your own worst enemy.

Life Lessons Learned (L3)

Take Good Care of Self and Others (TGCoSO)

Self	Others

01	02	03	04	05	06	07	08	09	10	11	12

I will feel great about today if:

Appointments	Intent	Action
7:00		
8:00		
9:00		
10:00		
11:00		
12:00		
1:00		
2:00		
3:00		
4:00		
5:00		
6:00		

Top three tasks and top priority for today

1.

2.

3.

01 02 03 04 05 06 07 08 09 10 11 12 13 14 15 16 17 18 19 20 21 22 23 24 25 26 27 28 29 30 31

Gratitudes

Today's self-awareness exercise

Today, give yourself permission to be imperfect. How did it go?

Life Lessons Learned (L3)

Take Good Care of Self and Others (TGCoSO)

Self	Others

01	02	03	04	05	06	07	08	09	10	11	12

I will feel great about today if:

Appointments	Intent	Action

7:00

8:00

9:00

10:00

11:00

12:00

1:00

2:00

3:00

4:00

5:00

6:00

Top three tasks and top priority for today

1.

2.

3.

01 02 03 04 05 06 07 08 09 10 11 12 13 14 15 16 17 18 19 20 21 22 23 24 25 26 27 28 29 30 31

Gratitudes

Today's self-awareness exercise

List songs that make you cry.

Life Lessons Learned (L3)

Take Good Care of Self and Others (TGCoSO)

Self	Others

I will feel great about today if:

Appointments	Intent	Action
7:00		
8:00		
9:00		
10:00		
11:00		
12:00		
1:00		
2:00		
3:00		
4:00		
5:00		
6:00		

Top three tasks and top priority for today

1.

2.

3.

Gratitudes

Today's self-awareness exercise
Ask a person who you respect who is at least 10 years older than yourself, what they do to keep strong in mind, body and spirit.

Life Lessons Learned (L3)

Take Good Care of Self and Others (TGCoSO)

Self	Others

| 01 | 02 | 03 | 04 | 05 | 06 | 07 | 08 | 09 | 10 | 11 | 12 |

I will feel great about today if:

Appointments	Intent	Action
7:00		
8:00		
9:00		
10:00		
11:00		
12:00		
1:00		
2:00		
3:00		
4:00		
5:00		
6:00		

Top three tasks and top priority for today

1.

2.

3.

Gratitudes

Today's self-awareness exercise

List songs that make you joyful.

Life Lessons Learned (L3)

Take Good Care of Self and Others (TGCoSO)

Self	Others

INTENTION

01	02	03	04	05	06	07	08	09	10	11	12

I will feel great about today if:

Appointments	Intent	Action
7:00		
8:00		
9:00		
10:00		
11:00		
12:00		
1:00		
2:00		
3:00		
4:00		
5:00		
6:00		

Top three tasks and top priority for today

1.

2.

3.

Gratitudes

Today's self-awareness exercise

Strike up a conversation with a complete stranger. What did you learn?

Life Lessons Learned (L3)

Take Good Care of Self and Others (TGCoSO)

Self	Others

I will feel great about today if:

Appointments	Intent	Action
7:00		
8:00		
9:00		
10:00		
11:00		
12:00		
1:00		
2:00		
3:00		
4:00		
5:00		
6:00		

Top three tasks and top priority for today

1.

2.

3.

01 02 03 04 05 06 07 08 09 10 11 12 13 14 15 16 17 18 19 20 21 22 23 24 25 26 27 28 29 30 31

Gratitudes

Today's self-awareness exercise

Today, try being good to others without seeking benefit for yourself.

Life Lessons Learned (L3)

Take Good Care of Self and Others (TGCoSO)

Self	Others

01	02	03	04	05	06	07	08	09	10	11	12

I will feel great about today if:

Appointments   Intent   Action

7:00

8:00

9:00

10:00

11:00

12:00

1:00

2:00

3:00

4:00

5:00

6:00

Top three tasks and top priority for today

1.

2.

3.

01 02 03 04 05 06 07 08 09 10 11 12 13 14 15 16 17 18 19 20 21 22 23 24 25 26 27 28 29 30 31

Gratitudes

Today's self-awareness exercise

List the positive qualities that make your body unique to you.

Life Lessons Learned (L3)

Take Good Care of Self and Others (TGCoSO)

Self	Others

I will feel great about today if:

Appointments	Intent	Action
7:00		
8:00		
9:00		
10:00		
11:00		
12:00		
1:00		
2:00		
3:00		
4:00		
5:00		
6:00		

Top three tasks and top priority for today

1.

2.

3.

01 02 03 04 05 06 07 08 09 10 11 12 13 14 15 16 17 18 19 20 21 22 23 24 25 26 27 28 29 30 31

Gratitudes

Today's self-awareness exercise

Reflect on one thing you could do today to take better care of yourself.

Life Lessons Learned (L3)

Take Good Care of Self and Others (TGCoSO)

Self	Others

| 01 | 02 | 03 | 04 | 05 | 06 | 07 | 08 | 09 | 10 | 11 | 12 |

I will feel great about today if:

Appointments **Intent** **Action**

7:00

8:00

9:00

10:00

11:00

12:00

1:00

2:00

3:00

4:00

5:00

6:00

Top three tasks and top priority for today

1.

2.

3.

01 02 03 04 05 06 07 08 09 10 11 12 13 14 15 16 17 18 19 20 21 22 23 24 25 26 27 28 29 30 31

Gratitudes

Today's self-awareness exercise

What positive changes could you make in the next week/month toward better self-care?

Life Lessons Learned (L3)

Take Good Care of Self and Others (TGCoSO)

Self	Others

01	02	03	04	05	06	07	08	09	10	11	12

I will feel great about today if:

Appointments   Intent   Action

7:00

8:00

9:00

10:00

11:00

12:00

1:00

2:00

3:00

4:00

5:00

6:00

Top three tasks and top priority for today

1.

2.

3.

Gratitudes

Today's self-awareness exercise

Today, work on managing your energy rather than your time.

Life Lessons Learned (L3)

Take Good Care of Self and Others (TGCoSO)

Self	Others

01	02	03	04	05	06	07	08	09	10	11	12

I will feel great about today if:

Appointments	Intent	Action
7:00		
8:00		
9:00		
10:00		
11:00		
12:00		
1:00		
2:00		
3:00		
4:00		
5:00		
6:00		

Top three tasks and top priority for today

1.

2.

3.

01 02 03 04 05 06 07 08 09 10 11 12 13 14 15 16 17 18 19 20 21 22 23 24 25 26 27 28 29 30 31

Gratitudes

Today's self-awareness exercise
Keep an energy journal so you can zero in on when you lose your energy and when it's at a peak.

Life Lessons Learned (L3)

Take Good Care of Self and Others (TGCoSO)

Self	Others

I will feel great about today if:

Appointments	Intent	Action
7:00		
8:00		
9:00		
10:00		
11:00		
12:00		
1:00		
2:00		
3:00		
4:00		
5:00		
6:00		

Top three tasks and top priority for today

1.

2.

3.

Gratitudes

Today's self-awareness exercise

Ask yourself what might be draining your energy.

Life Lessons Learned (L3)

Take Good Care of Self and Others (TGCoSO)

Self	Others

INTENTION

01	02	03	04	05	06	07	08	09	10	11	12

I will feel great about today if:

Appointments	Intent	Action
7:00		
8:00		
9:00		
10:00		
11:00		
12:00		
1:00		
2:00		
3:00		
4:00		
5:00		
6:00		

Top three tasks and top priority for today

1.

2.

3.

01 02 03 04 05 06 07 08 09 10 11 12 13 14 15 16 17 18 19 20 21 22 23 24 25 26 27 28 29 30 31

Gratitudes

Today's self-awareness exercise

Today, spend at least fifteen minutes on an activity that gives you a full sense of purpose.

Life Lessons Learned (L3)

Take Good Care of Self and Others (TGCoSO)

Self	Others

I will feel great about today if:

Appointments	Intent	Action
7:00		
8:00		
9:00		
10:00		
11:00		
12:00		
1:00		
2:00		
3:00		
4:00		
5:00		
6:00		

Top three tasks and top priority for today

1.

2.

3.

Gratitudes

Today's self-awareness exercise

Meditate or pray for fifteen minutes today.

Life Lessons Learned (L3)

Take Good Care of Self and Others (TGCoSO)

Self	Others

I will feel great about today if:

Appointments	Intent	Action
7:00		
8:00		
9:00		
10:00		
11:00		
12:00		
1:00		
2:00		
3:00		
4:00		
5:00		
6:00		

Top three tasks and top priority for today

1.

2.

3.

Gratitudes

Today's self-awareness exercise

Draw a pie chart showing where you want your time and energy to be going each day.

Life Lessons Learned (L3)

Take Good Care of Self and Others (TGCoSO)

Self	Others

| 01 | 02 | 03 | 04 | 05 | 06 | 07 | 08 | 09 | 10 | 11 | 12 |

I will feel great about today if:

Appointments	Intent	Action
7:00		
8:00		
9:00		
10:00		
11:00		
12:00		
1:00		
2:00		
3:00		
4:00		
5:00		
6:00		

Top three tasks and top priority for today

1.

2.

3.

01 02 03 04 05 06 07 08 09 10 11 12 13 14 15 16 17 18 19 20 21 22 23 24 25 26 27 28 29 30 31

Gratitudes

Today's self-awareness exercise

Draw a pie chart showing where your time and energy actually go every day.

Life Lessons Learned (L3)

Take Good Care of Self and Others (TGCoSO)

Self	Others

01	02	03	04	05	06	07	08	09	10	11	12

I will feel great about today if:

Appointments	Intent	Action
7:00		
8:00		
9:00		
10:00		
11:00		
12:00		
1:00		
2:00		
3:00		
4:00		
5:00		
6:00		

Top three tasks and top priority for today

1.

2.

3.

01 02 03 04 05 06 07 08 09 10 11 12 13 14 15 16 17 18 19 20 21 22 23 24 25 26 27 28 29 30 31

Gratitudes

Today's self-awareness exercise

Today, strive to understand HOW others are thinking about situations before you judge them.

Life Lessons Learned (L3)

Take Good Care of Self and Others (TGCoSO)

Self	Others

01	02	03	04	05	06	07	08	09	10	11	12

I will feel great about today if:

Appointments — Intent — Action

7:00

8:00

9:00

10:00

11:00

12:00

1:00

2:00

3:00

4:00

5:00

6:00

Top three tasks and top priority for today

1.

2.

3.

01 02 03 04 05 06 07 08 09 10 11 12 13 14 15 16 17 18 19 20 21 22 23 24 25 26 27 28 29 30 31

Gratitudes

Today's self-awareness exercise
Today, stop 'shoulding' on yourself (e.g. telling yourself you should be loved and approved of by everyone for everything you do).

Life Lessons Learned (L3)

Take Good Care of Self and Others (TGCoSO)

Self	Others

01	02	03	04	05	06	07	08	09	10	11	12

I will feel great about today if:

Appointments   Intent   Action

7:00

8:00

9:00

10:00

11:00

12:00

1:00

2:00

3:00

4:00

5:00

6:00

Top three tasks and top priority for today

1.

2.

3.

01 02 03 04 05 06 07 08 09 10 11 12 13 14 15 16 17 18 19 20 21 22 23 24 25 26 27 28 29 30 31

Gratitudes

Today's self-awareness exercise

Today, think about how your family relationships affects your emotions.

Life Lessons Learned (L3)

Take Good Care of Self and Others (TGCoSO)

Self	Others

01	02	03	04	05	06	07	08	09	10	11	12

I will feel great about today if:

Appointments	Intent	Action
7:00		
8:00		
9:00		
10:00		
11:00		
12:00		
1:00		
2:00		
3:00		
4:00		
5:00		
6:00		

Top three tasks and top priority for today

1.

2.

3.

Gratitudes

Today's self-awareness exercise
Look for ways to open up to current friends: Plan a trip or outing. Talk about something you usually might not be inclined to bring up.

Life Lessons Learned (L3)

Take Good Care of Self and Others (TGCoSO)

Self	Others

01	02	03	04	05	06	07	08	09	10	11	12

I will feel great about today if:

Appointments   Intent   Action

7:00

8:00

9:00

10:00

11:00

12:00

1:00

2:00

3:00

4:00

5:00

6:00

Top three tasks and top priority for today

1.

2.

3.

01 02 03 04 05 06 07 08 09 10 11 12 13 14 15 16 17 18 19 20 21 22 23 24 25 26 27 28 29 30 31

Gratitudes

Today's self-awareness exercise

Reconnect with an old friend today.

Life Lessons Learned (L3)

Take Good Care of Self and Others (TGCoSO)

Self	Others

01	02	03	04	05	06	07	08	09	10	11	12

I will feel great about today if:

Appointments	Intent	Action
7:00		
8:00		
9:00		
10:00		
11:00		
12:00		
1:00		
2:00		
3:00		
4:00		
5:00		
6:00		

Top three tasks and top priority for today

1.

2.

3.

Gratitudes

Today's self-awareness exercise
Identify the obstacles that tend to get in the way of your friendships: fear of rejection, unresolved conflicts, insufficient time, competitiveness, past failures.

Life Lessons Learned (L3)

Take Good Care of Self and Others (TGCoSO)

Self	Others

01	02	03	04	05	06	07	08	09	10	11	12

I will feel great about today if:

Appointments	Intent	Action
7:00		
8:00		
9:00		
10:00		
11:00		
12:00		
1:00		
2:00		
3:00		
4:00		
5:00		
6:00		

Top three tasks and top priority for today

1.

2.

3.

01 02 03 04 05 06 07 08 09 10 11 12 13 14 15 16 17 18 19 20 21 22 23 24 25 26 27 28 29 30 31

Gratitudes

Today's self-awareness exercise

Call one friend today and talk about something meaningful.

Life Lessons Learned (L3)

Take Good Care of Self and Others (TGCoSO)

Self	Others

01	02	03	04	05	06	07	08	09	10	11	12

I will feel great about today if:

Appointments   Intent   Action

7:00 ——————————   ——————————   ——————————

8:00 ——————————   ——————————   ——————————

9:00 ——————————   ——————————   ——————————

10:00 ——————————   ——————————   ——————————

11:00 ——————————   ——————————   ——————————

12:00 ——————————   ——————————   ——————————

1:00 ——————————   ——————————   ——————————

2:00 ——————————   ——————————   ——————————

3:00 ——————————   ——————————   ——————————

4:00 ——————————   ——————————   ——————————

5:00 ——————————   ——————————   ——————————

6:00 ——————————   ——————————   ——————————

Top three tasks and top priority for today

1. _____

2. _____

3. _____

01 02 03 04 05 06 07 08 09 10 11 12 13 14 15 16 17 18 19 20 21 22 23 24 25 26 27 28 29 30 31

Gratitudes

Today's self-awareness exercise

Today, keep track of your mood on an hourly basis. How does it change?

Life Lessons Learned (L3)

Take Good Care of Self and Others (TGCoSO)

Self	Others

01	02	03	04	05	06	07	08	09	10	11	12

I will feel great about today if:

Appointments	Intent	Action
7:00		
8:00		
9:00		
10:00		
11:00		
12:00		
1:00		
2:00		
3:00		
4:00		
5:00		
6:00		

Top three tasks and top priority for today

1. _____

2. _____

3. _____

01 02 03 04 05 06 07 08 09 10 11 12 13 14 15 16 17 18 19 20 21 22 23 24 25 26 27 28 29 30 31

Gratitudes

Today's self-awareness exercise

Try going all day without controlling someone else.

Life Lessons Learned (L3)

Take Good Care of Self and Others (TGCoSO)

Self	Others

| 01 | 02 | 03 | 04 | 05 | 06 | 07 | 08 | 09 | 10 | 11 | 12 |

I will feel great about today if:

Appointments	Intent	Action
7:00		
8:00		
9:00		
10:00		
11:00		
12:00		
1:00		
2:00		
3:00		
4:00		
5:00		
6:00		

Top three tasks and top priority for today

1.

2.

3.

Gratitudes

Today's self-awareness exercise

Today, list the things you want to change in your life.

Life Lessons Learned (L3)

Take Good Care of Self and Others (TGCoSO)

Self	Others

I will feel great about today if:

Appointments	Intent	Action
7:00		
8:00		
9:00		
10:00		
11:00		
12:00		
1:00		
2:00		
3:00		
4:00		
5:00		
6:00		

Top three tasks and top priority for today

1.

2.

3.

01 02 03 04 05 06 07 08 09 10 11 12 13 14 15 16 17 18 19 20 21 22 23 24 25 26 27 28 29 30 31

Gratitudes

Today's self-awareness exercise

Today, list the things you wish you could accept in your life.

Life Lessons Learned (L3)

Take Good Care of Self and Others (TGCoSO)

Self	Others

01	02	03	04	05	06	07	08	09	10	11	12

I will feel great about today if:

Appointments	Intent	Action
7:00		
8:00		
9:00		
10:00		
11:00		
12:00		
1:00		
2:00		
3:00		
4:00		
5:00		
6:00		

Top three tasks and top priority for today

1.

2.

3.

Gratitudes

Today's self-awareness exercise

Today, give people sincere compliments, see how it goes.

Life Lessons Learned (L3)

Take Good Care of Self and Others (TGCoSO)

Self	Others

01	02	03	04	05	06	07	08	09	10	11	12

I will feel great about today if:

Appointments	Intent	Action
7:00		
8:00		
9:00		
10:00		
11:00		
12:00		
1:00		
2:00		
3:00		
4:00		
5:00		
6:00		

Top three tasks and top priority for today

1.

2.

3.

Gratitudes

Today's self-awareness exercise

Today, reach out to someone you have been cut off from.

Life Lessons Learned (L3)

Take Good Care of Self and Others (TGCoSO)

Self	Others

I will feel great about today if:

Appointments	Intent	Action
7:00		
8:00		
9:00		
10:00		
11:00		
12:00		
1:00		
2:00		
3:00		
4:00		
5:00		
6:00		

Top three tasks and top priority for today

1.

2.

3.

Gratitudes

Today's self-awareness exercise

Try apologizing today without adding blame.

Life Lessons Learned (L3)

Take Good Care of Self and Others (TGCoSO)

Self	Others

01	02	03	04	05	06	07	08	09	10	11	12

I will feel great about today if:

Appointments	Intent	Action
7:00		
8:00		
9:00		
10:00		
11:00		
12:00		
1:00		
2:00		
3:00		
4:00		
5:00		
6:00		

Top three tasks and top priority for today

1.

2.

3.

Gratitudes

Today's self-awareness exercise
Write a letter to your younger self
https://www.theplayerstribune.com/category/letter-to-my-younger-self

Life Lessons Learned (L3)

Take Good Care of Self and Others (TGCoSO)

Self	Others

01	02	03	04	05	06	07	08	09	10	11	12

I will feel great about today if:

Appointments	Intent	Action
7:00		
8:00		
9:00		
10:00		
11:00		
12:00		
1:00		
2:00		
3:00		
4:00		
5:00		
6:00		

Top three tasks and top priority for today

1.

2.

3.

Gratitudes

Today's self-awareness exercise
Reflect on this quote. "The world tells us to seek success, power and money;
God tells us to seek humility, service and love" (Pope Francis, 2013)

Life Lessons Learned (L3)

Take Good Care of Self and Others (TGCoSO)

Self	Others

01	02	03	04	05	06	07	08	09	10	11	12

I will feel great about today if:

Appointments	Intent	Action
7:00		
8:00		
9:00		
10:00		
11:00		
12:00		
1:00		
2:00		
3:00		
4:00		
5:00		
6:00		

Top three tasks and top priority for today

1.
2.
3.

Gratitudes

Today's self-awareness exercise

Ask yourself why am I here on earth?

Life Lessons Learned (L3)

Take Good Care of Self and Others (TGCoSO)

Self	Others

01	02	03	04	05	06	07	08	09	10	11	12

I will feel great about today if:

Appointments   Intent   Action

7:00

8:00

9:00

10:00

11:00

12:00

1:00

2:00

3:00

4:00

5:00

6:00

Top three tasks and top priority for today

1.

2.

3.

01 02 03 04 05 06 07 08 09 10 11 12 13 14 15 16 17 18 19 20 21 22 23 24 25 26 27 28 29 30 31

Gratitudes

Today's self-awareness exercise

Ask yourself: What are the things that have driven me since I was a young adult?

Life Lessons Learned (L3)

Take Good Care of Self and Others (TGCoSO)

Self	Others

01	02	03	04	05	06	07	08	09	10	11	12

I will feel great about today if:

Appointments	Intent	Action
7:00		
8:00		
9:00		
10:00		
11:00		
12:00		
1:00		
2:00		
3:00		
4:00		
5:00		
6:00		

Top three tasks and top priority for today

1.

2.

3.

Gratitudes

Today's self-awareness exercise

Ask yourself what actions have I taken to further my mission?

Life Lessons Learned (L3)

Take Good Care of Self and Others (TGCoSO)

Self	Others

01	02	03	04	05	06	07	08	09	10	11	12

I will feel great about today if:

Appointments	Intent	Action
7:00		
8:00		
9:00		
10:00		
11:00		
12:00		
1:00		
2:00		
3:00		
4:00		
5:00		
6:00		

Top three tasks and top priority for today

1.

2.

3.

Gratitudes

Today's self-awareness exercise
Today, reflect on what this means to you "...be a little like the farmer who puts back into the soil what he takes out." Paul Newman

Life Lessons Learned (L3)

Take Good Care of Self and Others (TGCoSO)

Self	Others

| 01 | 02 | 03 | 04 | 05 | 06 | 07 | 08 | 09 | 10 | 11 | 12 |

I will feel great about today if:

Appointments	Intent	Action
7:00		
8:00		
9:00		
10:00		
11:00		
12:00		
1:00		
2:00		
3:00		
4:00		
5:00		
6:00		

Top three tasks and top priority for today

1.

2.

3.

01 02 03 04 05 06 07 08 09 10 11 12 13 14 15 16 17 18 19 20 21 22 23 24 25 26 27 28 29 30 31

Gratitudes

Today's self-awareness exercise
Reflect on this quote. "Real integrity is doing the right thing, knowing that nobody's going to know whether you did it or not." Oprah Winfrey

Life Lessons Learned (L3)

Take Good Care of Self and Others (TGCoSO)

Self	Others

| 01 | 02 | 03 | 04 | 05 | 06 | 07 | 08 | 09 | 10 | 11 | 12 |

I will feel great about today if:

Appointments	Intent	Action
7:00		
8:00		
9:00		
10:00		
11:00		
12:00		
1:00		
2:00		
3:00		
4:00		
5:00		
6:00		

Top three tasks and top priority for today

1.

2.

3.

01 02 03 04 05 06 07 08 09 10 11 12 13 14 15 16 17 18 19 20 21 22 23 24 25 26 27 28 29 30 31

Gratitudes

Today's self-awareness exercise
List the five core values by which you already are living your life.
(If you have three or seven, that's ok).

Life Lessons Learned (L3)

Take Good Care of Self and Others (TGCoSO)

Self	Others

I will feel great about today if:

Appointments	Intent	Action
7:00		
8:00		
9:00		
10:00		
11:00		
12:00		
1:00		
2:00		
3:00		
4:00		
5:00		
6:00		

Top three tasks and top priority for today

1. _____

2. _____

3. _____

Gratitudes

Today's self-awareness exercise

What's the best thing you have done in the last month, six months, and year?

Life Lessons Learned (L3)

Take Good Care of Self and Others (TGCoSO)

Self	Others

I will feel great about today if:

Appointments	Intent	Action
7:00		
8:00		
9:00		
10:00		
11:00		
12:00		
1:00		
2:00		
3:00		
4:00		
5:00		
6:00		

Top three tasks and top priority for today

1.

2.

3.

Gratitudes

Today's self-awareness exercise

Describe a great day.

Life Lessons Learned (L3)

Take Good Care of Self and Others (TGCoSO)

Self	Others

| 01 | 02 | 03 | 04 | 05 | 06 | 07 | 08 | 09 | 10 | 11 | 12 |

I will feel great about today if:

Appointments	Intent	Action
7:00		
8:00		
9:00		
10:00		
11:00		
12:00		
1:00		
2:00		
3:00		
4:00		
5:00		
6:00		

Top three tasks and top priority for today

1.

2.

3.

01 02 03 04 05 06 07 08 09 10 11 12 13 14 15 16 17 18 19 20 21 22 23 24 25 26 27 28 29 30 31

Gratitudes

Today's self-awareness exercise

What do you feel confident teaching someone else about?

Life Lessons Learned (L3)

Take Good Care of Self and Others (TGCoSO)

Self	Others

01	02	03	04	05	06	07	08	09	10	11	12

I will feel great about today if:

Appointments   Intent   Action

7:00

8:00

9:00

10:00

11:00

12:00

1:00

2:00

3:00

4:00

5:00

6:00

Top three tasks and top priority for today

1.

2.

3.

01 02 03 04 05 06 07 08 09 10 11 12 13 14 15 16 17 18 19 20 21 22 23 24 25 26 27 28 29 30 31

Gratitudes

Today's self-awareness exercise

Take the <u>Four Tendencies</u> quiz to learn more about yourself and others.

Life Lessons Learned (L3)

Take Good Care of Self and Others (TGCoSO)

Self	Others

| 01 | 02 | 03 | 04 | 05 | 06 | 07 | 08 | 09 | 10 | 11 | 12 |

I will feel great about today if:

Appointments	Intent	Action
7:00		
8:00		
9:00		
10:00		
11:00		
12:00		
1:00		
2:00		
3:00		
4:00		
5:00		
6:00		

Top three tasks and top priority for today

1.

2.

3.

Gratitudes

Today's self-awareness exercise
Today, try a few hours not multitasking. For example, don't listen to music when you walk to class.

Life Lessons Learned (L3)

Take Good Care of Self and Others (TGCoSO)

Self	Others

01	02	03	04	05	06	07	08	09	10	11	12

I will feel great about today if:

Appointments	Intent	Action
7:00		
8:00		
9:00		
10:00		
11:00		
12:00		
1:00		
2:00		
3:00		
4:00		
5:00		
6:00		

Top three tasks and top priority for today

1.
2.
3.

Gratitudes

Today's self-awareness exercise
Read something you find inspirational and write down what it means to you and why it is important.

Life Lessons Learned (L3)

Take Good Care of Self and Others (TGCoSO)

Self	Others

01	02	03	04	05	06	07	08	09	10	11	12

I will feel great about today if:

Appointments	Intent	Action
7:00		
8:00		
9:00		
10:00		
11:00		
12:00		
1:00		
2:00		
3:00		
4:00		
5:00		
6:00		

Top three tasks and top priority for today

1.

2.

3.

Gratitudes

Today's self-awareness exercise

Today, ask a classmate you do not know if there is anything you can do to help him/her.

Life Lessons Learned (L3)

Take Good Care of Self and Others (TGCoSO)

Self	Others

| 01 | 02 | 03 | 04 | 05 | 06 | 07 | 08 | 09 | 10 | 11 | 12 |

I will feel great about today if:

Appointments   **Intent**   **Action**

7:00 ————————— ————————— —————————

8:00 ————————— ————————— —————————

9:00 ————————— ————————— —————————

10:00 ———————— ————————— —————————

11:00 ———————— ————————— —————————

12:00 ———————— ————————— —————————

1:00 ————————— ————————— —————————

2:00 ————————— ————————— —————————

3:00 ————————— ————————— —————————

4:00 ————————— ————————— —————————

5:00 ————————— ————————— —————————

6:00 ————————— ————————— —————————

Top three tasks and top priority for today

1. _____

2. _____

3. _____

01 02 03 04 05 06 07 08 09 10 11 12 13 14 15 16 17 18 19 20 21 22 23 24 25 26 27 28 29 30 31

Gratitudes

Today's self-awareness exercise

Keep track of everything you eat and drink today.

Life Lessons Learned (L3)

_____

_____

_____

Take Good Care of Self and Others (TGCoSO)

Self	Others

I will feel great about today if:

Appointments   Intent   Action

7:00

8:00

9:00

10:00

11:00

12:00

1:00

2:00

3:00

4:00

5:00

6:00

Top three tasks and top priority for today

1.

2.

3.

01 02 03 04 05 06 07 08 09 10 11 12 13 14 15 16 17 18 19 20 21 22 23 24 25 26 27 28 29 30 31

Gratitudes

Today's self-awareness exercise

Think about what were your worries and fears at this time last year?

Life Lessons Learned (L3)

Take Good Care of Self and Others (TGCoSO)

Self	Others

I will feel great about today if:

Appointments	Intent	Action
7:00		
8:00		
9:00		
10:00		
11:00		
12:00		
1:00		
2:00		
3:00		
4:00		
5:00		
6:00		

Top three tasks and top priority for today

1.

2.

3.

Gratitudes

Today's self-awareness exercise

Today, go to a museum or art gallery and reflect on what you see.

Life Lessons Learned (L3)

Take Good Care of Self and Others (TGCoSO)

Self	Others

01	02	03	04	05	06	07	08	09	10	11	12

I will feel great about today if:

Appointments   Intent   Action

7:00

8:00

9:00

10:00

11:00

12:00

1:00

2:00

3:00

4:00

5:00

6:00

Top three tasks and top priority for today

1.

2.

3.

01 02 03 04 05 06 07 08 09 10 11 12 13 14 15 16 17 18 19 20 21 22 23 24 25 26 27 28 29 30 31

Gratitudes

Today's self-awareness exercise

Draw a cartoon or picture today representing anything you choose.

Life Lessons Learned (L3)

Take Good Care of Self and Others (TGCoSO)

Self	Others

01	02	03	04	05	06	07	08	09	10	11	12

I will feel great about today if:

Appointments	Intent	Action
7:00		
8:00		
9:00		
10:00		
11:00		
12:00		
1:00		
2:00		
3:00		
4:00		
5:00		
6:00		

Top three tasks and top priority for today

1.

2.

3.

01 02 03 04 05 06 07 08 09 10 11 12 13 14 15 16 17 18 19 20 21 22 23 24 25 26 27 28 29 30 31

Gratitudes

Today's self-awareness exercise

Reflect, and then write down, what you want as your professional life.

Life Lessons Learned (L3)

Take Good Care of Self and Others (TGCoSO)

Self	Others

INTENTION

| 01 | 02 | 03 | 04 | 05 | 06 | 07 | 08 | 09 | 10 | 11 | 12 |

I will feel great about today if:

Appointments	Intent	Action
7:00		
8:00		
9:00		
10:00		
11:00		
12:00		
1:00		
2:00		
3:00		
4:00		
5:00		
6:00		

Top three tasks and top priority for today

1.

2.

3.

01 02 03 04 05 06 07 08 09 10 11 12 13 14 15 16 17 18 19 20 21 22 23 24 25 26 27 28 29 30 31

Gratitudes

Today's self-awareness exercise

Write your plan for tomorrow and review it the day after tomorrow.

Life Lessons Learned (L3)

Take Good Care of Self and Others (TGCoSO)

Self	Others

01	02	03	04	05	06	07	08	09	10	11	12

I will feel great about today if:

Appointments	Intent	Action
7:00		
8:00		
9:00		
10:00		
11:00		
12:00		
1:00		
2:00		
3:00		
4:00		
5:00		
6:00		

Top three tasks and top priority for today

1.

2.

3.

Gratitudes

Today's self-awareness exercise

What movies affected you to the point of influencing your life. Why?

Life Lessons Learned (L3)

Take Good Care of Self and Others (TGCoSO)

Self	Others

01	02	03	04	05	06	07	08	09	10	11	12

I will feel great about today if:

Appointments	Intent	Action
7:00		
8:00		
9:00		
10:00		
11:00		
12:00		
1:00		
2:00		
3:00		
4:00		
5:00		
6:00		

Top three tasks and top priority for today

1.

2.

3.

01 02 03 04 05 06 07 08 09 10 11 12 13 14 15 16 17 18 19 20 21 22 23 24 25 26 27 28 29 30 31

Gratitudes

Today's self-awareness exercise

Name a memorable experience with each parent.

Life Lessons Learned (L3)

Take Good Care of Self and Others (TGCoSO)

Self	Others

01	02	03	04	05	06	07	08	09	10	11	12

I will feel great about today if:

Appointments	Intent	Action
7:00		
8:00		
9:00		
10:00		
11:00		
12:00		
1:00		
2:00		
3:00		
4:00		
5:00		
6:00		

Top three tasks and top priority for today

1.

2.

3.

01 02 03 04 05 06 07 08 09 10 11 12 13 14 15 16 17 18 19 20 21 22 23 24 25 26 27 28 29 30 31

Gratitudes

Today's self-awareness exercise

"I arise in the morning torn between a desire to improve (or save) the world and a desire to enjoy (or savor) the world. This makes it hard to plan the day."–E.B. White.
What does this mean to you?

Life Lessons Learned (L3)

Take Good Care of Self and Others (TGCoSO)

Self	Others

| 01 | 02 | 03 | 04 | 05 | 06 | 07 | 08 | 09 | 10 | 11 | 12 |

I will feel great about today if:

Appointments	Intent	Action
7:00		
8:00		
9:00		
10:00		
11:00		
12:00		
1:00		
2:00		
3:00		
4:00		
5:00		
6:00		

Top three tasks and top priority for today

1.

2.

3.

01 02 03 04 05 06 07 08 09 10 11 12 13 14 15 16 17 18 19 20 21 22 23 24 25 26 27 28 29 30 31

Gratitudes

Today's self-awareness exercise

Reflect on how much money is enough.

Life Lessons Learned (L3)

Take Good Care of Self and Others (TGCoSO)

Self	Others

I will feel great about today if:

Appointments	Intent	Action
7:00		
8:00		
9:00		
10:00		
11:00		
12:00		
1:00		
2:00		
3:00		
4:00		
5:00		
6:00		

Top three tasks and top priority for today

1.

2.

3.

01 02 03 04 05 06 07 08 09 10 11 12 13 14 15 16 17 18 19 20 21 22 23 24 25 26 27 28 29 30 31

Gratitudes

Today's self-awareness exercise

Imagine yourself five years from now. What do you see?

Life Lessons Learned (L3)

Take Good Care of Self and Others (TGCoSO)

Self	Others

I will feel great about today if:

Appointments	Intent	Action
7:00		
8:00		
9:00		
10:00		
11:00		
12:00		
1:00		
2:00		
3:00		
4:00		
5:00		
6:00		

Top three tasks and top priority for today

1.

2.

3.

01 02 03 04 05 06 07 08 09 10 11 12 13 14 15 16 17 18 19 20 21 22 23 24 25 26 27 28 29 30 31

Gratitudes

Today's self-awareness exercise

What's your personal hashtag? For example #livewithjoy

Life Lessons Learned (L3)

Take Good Care of Self and Others (TGCoSO)

Self	Others

I will feel great about today if:

Appointments   Intent   Action

7:00 ———————————   ———————————   ———————————

8:00 ———————————   ———————————   ———————————

9:00 ———————————   ———————————   ———————————

10:00 ———————————   ———————————   ———————————

11:00 ———————————   ———————————   ———————————

12:00 ———————————   ———————————   ———————————

1:00 ———————————   ———————————   ———————————

2:00 ———————————   ———————————   ———————————

3:00 ———————————   ———————————   ———————————

4:00 ———————————   ———————————   ———————————

5:00 ———————————   ———————————   ———————————

6:00 ———————————   ———————————   ———————————

Top three tasks and top priority for today

1. ———————————————————————————————

2. ———————————————————————————————

3. ———————————————————————————————

01 02 03 04 05 06 07 08 09 10 11 12 13 14 15 16 17 18 19 20 21 22 23 24 25 26 27 28 29 30 31

Gratitudes

Today's self-awareness exercise

Think about one of your favorite mentors. What was it about that person that you admire?

Life Lessons Learned (L3)

Take Good Care of Self and Others (TGCoSO)

Self	Others

Looking Forward

Thank you for participating in the process. Next I will ask you to re-do your goals, based on everything you have learned about yourself from going through the courageous process of filling out the journal. Reflect on lessons learned during the ninety-one days. Consider what made you grateful. What did you learn from the assessments that you took? What did you learn about Self-care from the Section on taking good care of yourself and others? What did you learn from the Lessons Learned section?

Go back to the goals that you wrote at the beginning of the journal. Did you achieve them? How? Where did you fall short? Why?

Now set new specific short-term goals that align with all you learned about yourself. Use the process I describe below to write your new ninety day, one year, and three year goals.

You might try a method I have used for five decades: write each goal on an index card using the following format:

What is the goal?
Describe the specific, measurable goals you want to achieve.

By when?
Set a deadline for achieving your goal.

Why?
Explain why this goal is important to you personally. What core values are central to this goal? What passions will you be able to engage working toward this goal? How is this goal grounded in your mission?

How?
Briefly describe i how you will achieve this goal. How do your strengths align with this goal?

Support?
One of the myths that people often hold dear is that they are solely responsible for their own success. But today, there is more and more acceptance of the notion that if you are going to succeed, it will be within a community, a group of other committed individuals. What support do you need from others to achieve this goal, and how will you get it? Who will be on your goal achievement team?

Goals

90 Days

School Career Goals

Personal Goals

1 Year

School Career Goals

Personal Goals

3 Year

School Career Goals

Personal Goals

Pasick Personal Leadership Development Plan

Key Strengths from Gallup & Best Self Exercises	Your Key Relationships
1	
2	
3	
4	
5	

Your Interests & Passions	Your Mission & Values

Personality	Blind Spots

Your Energy & Body	
1	
2	
3	
4	
5	

Your Mind	
1	
2	
3	
4	
5	

Next 3 Months: Work Goal	1 Year: Work Goal	3-5 Year: Work Goal
What? When? Why? How? With Whom?		
Next 3 Months: Personal Goal	1 Year: Personal Goal	3-5 Year: Personal Goal
What? When? Why? How? With Whom?		
Next 3 Months: Health Goal	1 Year: Health Goal	3-5 Year: Health Goal
What? When? Why? How? With Whom?		
Next 3 Months: Goal #4	1 Year: Goal #4	3-5 Year: Goal #4
What? When? Why? How? With Whom?		
Next 3 Months: Goal #5	1 Year: Goal #5	3-5 Year: Goal #5
What? When? Why? How? With Whom?		

....

Conclusion

....

Congratulations on your work on improving yourself through gaining an increased sense of self-awareness. Please keep in touch and let me know how I can help you on your journey.

You can reach me at Rob@robpasick.com or visiting my site, robpasick.com. Be sure to request my weekly Dr. Rob Tips newsletter.

Special thank you to Melissa Odegaard for designing this Journal.